I WANT TO SEE YOU SHINING: THE GUIDE

A HANDBOOK FOR MANAGING
THE STRESS AND ANXIETY OF PANDEMICS,
PROTESTS, AND PAIN

MARK BATSON AND
DR. ALFIEE M. BRELAND-NOBLE

CONTENTS

MANAGING STRESS IN THE PANDEMIC

The definition of pandemic is "an epidemic occurring worldwide, or over a very wide area crossing international boundaries and usually affecting a large number of people." The word reeks with fear. It seems like an invisible and giant monster that has taken something already as terrifying as an epidemic and magnified it to extreme proportions, inescapable, sure to kill us all one day.

Recently, I asked a younger family member what the word "pandemic" meant. She replied, "A pandemic means everybody's going to get it and it's the end of the world."

Every day we hear reports of massive hospitalizations and deaths, and every day we share that amplified sense of an invisible killer that creeps around and attacks the most vulnerable of our friends and family members. Every day we are all aware of our own fears of this monster entering our own circles and changing our worlds.

I wanted to create this book as a reply to those who said, "You need to deal with it," when I confessed that I was facing a problem or difficulty of some sort. In my mind I always asked, "What does 'deal with it' mean?"

This booklet is designed with you in mind. We want to support you fully and uniquely so we designed this booklet to care for your mental health and emotional needs during this unprecedented time. We have come together as a team: a world-renowned musician and music producer and an internationally recognized psychologist, scientist and media personality expert in mental health for diverse people. It is no coincidence that we are also both Howard University Bison deeply committed to the lived experiences of Black people of the diaspora. Stay with us, as we explore the emotional issues unique to this period in time and provide our ideas on how you can take care of your most important asset, You.

—Dr. Alfiee

HEARING OF THE DEATH OF A FRIEND'S LOVED ONE

When a person you are close with reports the death of a loved one, they can often be in a highly emotional state, crying or extremely agitated with pain. This is definitely not the time to say "Deal with it." As empathetic humans, it is our natural response to join them in their grief.

During the pandemic, I received calls from one of my best friends in Los Angeles to report the sudden death of his father from COVID-19, as well as the passing of one of my sister's closest friends.

Both calls pushed my own emotions to the surface, as I sought to control them so that I could be supportive of the sadness of these persons that I love. After each call, I went about my day not acknowledging that I was affected by their losses. As time progressed, I knew that was im-possible: the pain of those I love is my pain as well. I was going to have to acknowledge my own emotional responses, account for them, and then make a plan of action to stay on top of them.

What to Do

1. *Acknowledge and name the loss. Sometimes we may want to avoid the reality of losing someone we love.*

1. *It is important to actively resist this urge, even if it feels like the only way to get through the sadness. This is not to say that you need to grieve in any specific way, it is only to share*

with you that just naming the issue is the key first step.

1. *Be patient with yourself. Don't look around and expect your grief to operate on any timeline other than your own. Some people grieve for a few months, others for years. These are both okay. You must do what works for you and you alone.*

2. *Eastern philosophy and beliefs on death teach us that mourning carries with it a way to honor those who have come before us. I learned this from Dr. Helen Hsu of Stanford University, the lead mental health consultant on the Netflix show 13 Reasons Why.*

3. *Try adding a mantra to your daily routine. This album offers many beautiful songs that can help you with this process as well. My favorite for a time like this is "You Are Elegant."*

— Dr. Alfiee

SADNESS AND ANXIETY
MANTRA 1

One of the first things you can do after hearing unfortunate news is take a few deep breaths and say the words "I am safe."

I AM SAFE

I AM SAFE

I AM SAFE

Repeat again while taking deep breaths. Take a moment to become aware of your breathing.

Those words can be repeated over and over again, until you begin to focus on the two most important things at that particular moment: your own safety and your own breathing.

As you examine your own present reality, you can often find that even if your level of anxiety, fear, or sadness is increasing, your own world is the only thing you can really control.

Breathing can be the most important item on your present agenda, and after repeating "I am safe" for a minute you can move on to these words:

I AM ENJOYING MY BREATHING

I AM ENJOYING MY BREATHING

I AM ENJOYING MY BREATHING

When you travel on a plane, the flight attendants always instruct you that during an in-flight crisis, When you travel on a plane, the flight attendants always instruct you that during an in-flight crisis, if the oxygen masks are released, you should put yours on first before beginning to administer aid to others. This is an ideal example for what you should do in a crisis situation: examine your own stress levels, anxiety, your breathing, and so on. Check in with yourself. Assess where and how you are at that moment. Do some focus work to get yourself together. With that oxygen mask on, metaphorically speaking, you can now help your friends and family. Without you taking care of you, you are not going to be what is needed from others. Take whatever time you need to ground and refocus yourself before moving on to the next order of business: addressing the anxiety and sadness that have now entered your world. Assess where and how you are at that moment. Do some focus work to get yourself together. With that oxygen mask on, metaphorically speaking, you can now help your friends and family. Without you taking care of you, you are not going to be what is needed from others. Take whatever time you need to ground and refocus yourself before moving on to the next order of business: addressing the anxiety and sadness that have now entered your world.

BEING UNABLE TO GO TO HOSPITALS
TO SEE LOVED ONES WHO ARE SICK

A few months into the COVID pandemic, I got a call from my mom telling me that the neighbor across the street from her was taken to the hospital in the middle of the night. She watched in fear as the EMS workers put the elderly woman on a stretcher and took her away, as the poor woman's daughters watched on the street, unable to accompany their mother to the hospital, which they definitely would have done under any other circumstance.

Fortunately, the woman survived the hospital visit and returned home a few days later. This made me realize that if a person passes away only one time, there's no sense in driving the person's family into a mentally frantic state with every crisis, spreading the sickness of stress and its assault on our nervous system.

We must always expect the best and prepare for the worst. However, in these moments of panic and crisis, it is important to keep thinking positively, since that uplifting energy can also be shared with the person you are afraid for.

You can try breathing, being aware of your breathing, and using this mantra:

EVERYTHING WILL WORK OUT
FOR THE BEST
EVERYTHING WILL WORK OUT
FOR THE BEST
EVERYTHING WILL WORK OUT
FOR THE BEST

Of course, everything may not always work out for the best, but mourning a person's death multiple times before it happens is not going to work out for the best for anyone. Knowing that a loved one is in he hospital alone, hurting, possibly crying and terrified and in need of attention, can be a heartbreaking experience. Sending them loving energy while anticipating their recovery is one of the things we can do to manage our own stress during a tough situation like this.

I AM EXPECTING GOOD NEWS

I AM EXPECTING GOOD NEWS

I AM EXPECTING GOOD NEWS

Relax. Put a healthy image of the person in your head. Look at a photograph or some other reminder of a happy time you've had together, and project that these happy times will be coming again. The only thing we really have is the present and the moment, and if the person is still alive there is a lot there to be thankful for.

I AM THANKFUL THAT I CAN STILL SPEAK WITH _____

I AM THANKFUL THAT I CAN STILL SPEAK WITH _____

I AM THANKFUL THAT I CAN STILL SPEAK WITH _____

Always remember that our bodies have a fight-or-flight response, and in a crisis we produce an extraordinary amount of adrenalin and other chemicals into our system that over the long term can be extremely dangerous. What we never want to happen is that our own stress levels get so high that we're the ones riding the ambulance to the hospital for treatment, causing even more panic within a household. Emotionally reliving a cataclysmic moment repeatedly can wreak havoc on your body and mind.

Singing, humming, or chanting can also be a great tool to manage stress during an encounter like this. Singing activates the vagus nerve, the longest cranial nerve in the body. It connects the brain, stomach, lungs and heart. This nerve plays a critical role in helping us to digest food and to rest

Increasing the tone of the vagus nerve has proved to be a way to enable our bodies to relax faster when experiencing stressful encounters. The vagus nerve is also connected to your vocal cords and throat muscles. The practice of humming, singing, and changing relieves stress in humans. They have done so for as long as we have been human, and they are powerful, natu-ral tools to use today. Singing can help you anticipate a best possible scenario and manage your emotions during a worst-possible scenario.

Here are some other ideas for you to consider.

1. *Remember that you can only control what you do. Your mental health depends on your reduc-ing the number of unchecked stressors in your life. So use some of the tips we've shared to help you reduce your stress and manage it better.*

2. *Be creative in how you engage loved ones who are sick. This will help you feel a bit more empowered in doing "something," even if you can't get to the hospital. For example, you might coordinate daily follow-up with hospital staff where you agree to make yourself available at the same time each weekday for a call.*

3. *Connect with family who are not in the hospital to support the family member or loved one who is. Agree to get together to pray or meditate weekly. Organize a virtual get-well-card making party. Make a playlist for your loved one in the hospital with a song apiece from each of a few close family members.*

A song I like for these instances is "I Am" (which helps me set my intention on what I can control).

—*Dr. Alfiee*

SOME NEXT STEPS TO
MASTER FEAR

On the song "Mastering Fear," I created a three-part fear mantra that challenges fear and takes it on directly.

I AM STRONG AND COURA GEOUS
I'M ABOVE FEAR

This affirmation acknowledges first that fear does exist. So often we hear people say, "I ain't afraid of nothing," when deep in our hearts, we are well aware that fear is a natural human emotion, and that facing or experiencing it is absolutely normal. It is what we do with it that counts.

I AM STRONG AND COURA GEOUS
I CONTROL FEAR

This affirmation puts fear under our direction. Fear now obeys us, rather than the other way around. Controlling fear allows a person who has risen above it to now take the reins.

I AM STRONG AND COURAGEOUS
I HAVE NO FEAR

This is the final step in the affirmation, reaching the top of the mountain. You have mastered the fear and are now ready to face and work the problem or situation.

Now combine them:

I AM STRONG AND COURAGEOUS
I'M ABOVE FEAR

I AM STRONG AND COURAGEOUS
I CONTROL FEAR

I AM STRONG AND COURAGEOUS
I HAVE NO FEAR

I AM STRONG AND COURAGEOUS
I HAVE NO FEAR

I AM STRONG AND COURAGEOUS
I HAVE NO FEAR

Saying this mantra in the mirror really helped me manage the fear of the first few months of the pandemic.

HEARING OF THE SICKNESS OR DEATH
OF A FRIEND OR FAMILY MEMBER

Often the death of someone close to us not only can create extreme sadness for the loss of their physical presence on this earth, but it also can make us examine our own mortality.

I AM MORE THAN THIS FLESH
AND BODY
I AM SPIRIT AND SPIRIT IS
IMMORTAL
I AM BLESSED TO BE ALIVE

As time progresses, we will age, and our bodies and minds will behave differently. Many people will experience huge changes in their movement and daily pains in their joints and limbs. As we experience these losses and challenges, it is essential that we hold onto our beliefs. Many of these ideals are cherished in the major religions as well as in the spiritual community.

We believe that our bodies are for now, and our spirits are for eternity.

While embracing these ideas, it is clear to see that our loved ones who are passing into eternity have moved forward into their most divine state. They have become as dreams, more beau-tiful than anything we could possibly imagine.

If we are to believe in a spiritual afterlife, we are saying that our few decades on this planet are nothing compared to the vastness of time that encompasses our lives in the spiritual realm. Will you be in this new heavenly place of no physical limitations for a hundred years, thousands of years, or more? These are questions that we cannot answer in this lifetime.

They will be answered only on the day we walk through that divine door to eternity.

For now, though, we can acknowledge that our loved ones have become more beautiful, more powerful, and more capable than during their time on Earth, that they have gathered a storehouse of emotions and experiences and brought them to a source of energy so powerful that they will enjoy us and everything they have learned while living on earth for eternity. Or perhaps, as Buddhism and Hinduism teach, they will decide to return to this plane to learn and grow more.

With that thought, it can be releasing to take a picture of your loved one, light candles in your own memorial, give thanks to the universe for every second that you had them in your circle of communication, and then make a statement that although they have returned to the universe, they have returned to a beauty that will only increase as time progresses.

You are beautiful, more beautiful
with every second
You are beautiful, more beautiful
with every second
You are beautiful, more beautiful
with every second

It is important that we also recognize the beauty of aging and our progress until our spirits are released from our bodies, and we become as powerful as our dreams.

I AM BEAUTIFUL, MORE BEAUTIFUL WITH
EVERY SECOND
I AM BEAUTIFUL, MORE BEAUTIFUL WITH
EVERY SECOND
I AM BEAUTIFUL, MORE BEAUTIFUL WITH
EVERY SECOND

If you say a person's name out loud and speak of them, they will always be there in a spiritual capacity. As humans, we are blessed with powerful imaginations, and we have creative, beautiful ways to experience the people we love with our minds.

No one ever is gone. They may not be physically among us, but then again, they can be always be hugged in your dreams or in your creative mind. Perhaps Whitney Houston sang this next mantra best,

It is also important to know that it is okay to grieve, it is okay to cry. In fact, crying is very healthy for the body. It not only releases pent-up emotions but can also clear the lungs and nasal passages of unwanted mucus and bacteria. Feel free to let it all out, to remove the sadness from your body and place it outside. Find an enclosed or private place if you need to scream.

I WILL ALWAYS LOVE YOU
I WILL ALWAYS LOVE YOU
I WILL ALWAYS LOVE YOU

Here are some steps you can take in order to take control of or manage your fear or grief.

1. Determine if you are worried about this moment in time or if this is part of a larger pattern of worry for you. Do you find that even when nothing is outwardly "wrong" you still worry? Do you experience things like racing thoughts, uneasiness, upset stomach, sweaty palms, or a sense that "the other shoe is about to drop"?

2. If this feels like your life, you may be experi-encing anxiety, and we want to support you.

3. Some ways you can work on managing anxiety:

   a. Recognize that it is a real illness.

   b. Read about it so you can learn more.

   c. Take some time to breathe— and just zone out—even if it is just for a few minutes.

   d. Listen to this album to give you calming vibes.

I love these songs to help bring me back to a place of peace; "Celebrate the Victory" and "Shining at 528 Hz."

—Dr. Alfiee

BEING QUARANTINED ALONE OR IN A SMALL SPACE WITH MULTIPLE PEOPLE

The current pandemic makes demands on all of us, but especially those who value their privacy and are now called upon to share their space with people whom they know and love. Let's face it: even our most loved ones can sometimes get on our nerves, and in the spirit of putting that oxygen mask on, sometimes we have to take care of ourselves before we pop. The opposite can be true, though: in some instances, we've been tucked away in our own cocoons, unable to visit with our friends and loved ones, alone. There's only so much Netflix. How do we keep ourselves from getting cabin fever? Let Dr. Alfiee point out a few strategies in the column to the right.

The trickiest thing about this latest pandemic is the ability of the coronavirus to hunt when people need to be together, share hugs, and grieve collectively.

1. Carve out some space just for you. If you are in a cramped space, for example, maybe wake up before everyone else in the house and camp out in the kitchen for 15 minutes or so of alone time.

2. Create a routine that prioritizes your mental health, and stick with it. You can start out with something small like buying a mindfulness coloring book. Color in it for three minutes three times a week, building up to regular intervals and adding more coloring time as you wish.

2. Sit down with your family and have an honest conversation about what you need to stay mentally safe and healthy during this time. They may have ideas for you!

Go back to the song "Affirmations" to reaffirm that you are ok and that you are fearfully and wonderfully made.

—Dr. Alfiee

BEING UNABLE TO ATTEND FUNERALS

I never thought we would see the day where appreciation for funerals has grown exponentially, but these days, we are often delegated with the responsibility to grieve without closure and are not able to be comforted by our family members. How are we supposed to move on without saying goodbye?

Perhaps this is a time to create our own personal rituals. Of course, we can use services like Zoom to gather and share good vibes and energy, but there is nothing like being there in person, to cry, laugh, and share hugs.

Perhaps this is a time to create our own personal rituals. Of course, we can use services like Zoom to gather and share good vibes and energy, but there is nothing like being there in person, to cry, laugh, and share hugs.

This is where working in your own creative space can be of help.

I AM BLESSED TO HAVE HAD TIME TO BE WITH YOU IN THIS DIMENSION AND IN THIS WORLD.

I WILL ALWAYS CHERISH EVERY MOMENT THAT YOU WERE IN MY CIRCLE AND SPACE, AND I PROMISE TO HONOR YOUR MEMORY.

I KNOW THAT YOU HAVE ASCENDED TO SOMETHING FAR GREATER THAN HERE, AND I CONGRATULATE YOU ON ACHIEVING A DIVINE AND ETERNAL FORM.

I WILL CRY FOR YOU.
I WILL LAUGH FOR YOU.
I WILL LIVE ON FOR YOU.

After reciting this meditation, make a mental image of the person you love rising up, ascending into the Universe, and becoming one with the stars.

They have become one of the billions of stars in the sky, and they are all-powerful in their essence.

As they rise into the clouds, give thanks, again and again. Say thank you, thank you, thank you, thank you . . . you are blessed.

After blowing out the candles, the ritual is complete. You can either meditate after, have a meal, or even call some friends to talk good thoughts about the deliverance of a divine spirit into the cosmos.

MANAGING THE RACIAL DISPARITIES IN COVID-19 VICTIMS

When the coronavirus first manifested and began to take hold, I sat with my partner in the early stages as we watched the reports from China and then Italy that said that mostly elderly people and those with preexisting conditions were the ones who were losing their lives. I talked with loved ones, remembering that AIDS was at first a gay disease, but as time progressed, it became the killer of 25 million

Africans and then into the person-of-color disease it is perceived to be when you watch HIV medicine commercials on television today. AIDS went from a gay disease in Greenwich Village and San Francisco to one that now kills a million people a year in Africa.

Being Black, I find it necessary to address concerns of racial attacks within the confines and structures of government programs. After all, if the US government could personally and directly sponsor and endorse and legalize the rape, torture, and murder during slavery of African Americans, Jim Crow laws that sanctioned legal torture and murder and lynchings of Black people who wanted equality, and real estate redlining that blocked Blacks from buying property, and mass incarceration sending Black people disproportionately to prison for the same crimes as whites, is it not possible that that very government is using bioweapons to attack the Black population?

As a historical student of everything from the Tuskegee experiments to COINTELPRO to poisoned blankets given to Native Americans, I think that it is reasonable to have concerns about whether or not COVID-19 was a focused attack. In the early stages of COVID, after all, Americans first were presented with news reports saying that not only was the disease focused on the elderly and previously ill, but for some reason, it was also nonexistent in Africa. Black people let out a sigh of relief, only to have that comforting breath sucked in and held in our collective chests a few months later with new reports that now acknowledged that Black people were three to five times more likely to catch and die from the disease than any other race.

Today, African American deaths from COVID-19 are now being charted at double the percentage rate of the demographic of races, along with Latin Americans, as White people stay mostly below their demographic numbers on the death scale. Meanwhile, Africa has just logged in a million COVID infections, and Brazil, with its large Black population, has joined them. We all know that typically, Africans and those of African descent have fewer options in the healthcare community, but at the same time, we are also hearing the the words "plandemic" being used in small circles, as many African Americans have no choice but to wonder if something fishy is going on. As we all know, there are plenty of elderly, overweight people with preexisting conditions of every race, and it is logical to

it is logical to wonder why African Americans have been singled out by a virus that has no eyes or ears and a seemingly focused method of attack. We ask ourselves, why is the coronavirus doing the most damage in nations that have

African and African-descended populations? What can we do? What can we do to suppress the anger from the history of past attacks that links the current pandemic to our history?

I have read many analyses and heard many conspiracy theories. The one thing we are sure of now is that no one has any answers or solutions. Some days we hear that Vitamin D is the solution, since people with brown skin need to spend that much more time in the sun to absorb the necessary Vitamin D to fight the virus. The next day we hear government press conferences that advise the possibility of injecting disinfectants or untested drugs. We hear the names Dr. Fauci and Bill Gates linked to more conspiracies, but in the end, we all have no answers, and are left with our own minds and perceptions on how to proceed.

The news that African Americans are dying disproportionately touched me on a lightning-bolt level. In some ways, it linked hundreds of years of history to this one event, and even if I could not prove what the intentions were, my DNA full of African persecution was already answering for me. I was afraid, but even more so, I was angry and felt powerless. If this was an attack, what could I do about it? The answer was: nothing. Anyone who mentioned their history in links to the present would be perceived as possibly crazy, losing it, or wearing a tinfoil hat. I knew it was best to keep my

my mouth shut when linking the coronavirus to hundreds of years of African American suffering in the United States.

I began to write: something to feel powerful, something to feel like I could not be harmed, something to feel like I could take this beast on and defeat it soundly.

I decided that I would fight back with water, with vegetables, with fruits, on my treadmill walking, running, lifting weights, and do anything I could to make my consciousness into a force that could not be defeated by anything.

I AM

I'm a walking monument to excellence
I'm a higher force of being
I'm the pinnacle of universal intelligence
I'm the living biblical testament

It's not arrogance when you're living proof of the
evidence
When the God force surrounds you and you
fulfilled all the prerequisites

I now admonish decadence and make a new
precedent

My body is full of life force and now higher forces
are blessing it
The holy spirit refreshing it
I'm feeling it all up inside of my chest and s***

There's no energy that can defeat me, beat me, sit me
down or hold me back All attacks are like Neo when
he waved them bullets,
Devils is shooting at me crooked and shocked to see
me still standing Grandmaster Commanding with
enough passion to fill up the Grand Canyon

COPING WITH RACIAL STRIFE

Growing up in Bushwick projects in Brooklyn during the years of extremely high murder counts, I can attest to the tricky negotiation of safety that an honest, hardworking Black man, woman, or child must undergo every day.

Like everywhere, there are crime and criminals in our community, but the most difficult part is walking the line between criminals who see you as prey and police officers who see you as yet another criminal.

As a 6'2" Black man who weighs more than two hundred pounds, I can tell you personally of the fear that is generated by my presence alone, and the results it can sometimes cause with the police.

My first experience in stop-and-frisk profiling came when I was coming back from the grocery store with a few friends. I was about eight years old. The three of us were crossing the street when a Black cop walked up with an elderly woman who pointed us out—for what I still don't know. The cop put us up against a fence, searched us, and went through our pockets, asking about a crime perpetrated against the woman. A small crowd from the neighborhood gathered to observe the show, but we were eventually let go. My mother went to the police station and filed an extensive report. She was extremely politically active in those days and was willing to go all the way to fight for her and our rights. Later that week, we saw that cop again in the middle of the street directing traffic. At least in those days there was some type of reprimand that the entire community could feel relief from.

A few years later I was in Chicago visiting my cousins. There were four of us coming home from a movie. We had just gotten off the train and were standing on the platform of the El when a woman walked up with two cops. There it was again: "There they go, right there, officer!" The first cop sprang into action, telling us all to get against the platform. My cousin moved a little bit, and the cop grabbed his ankle and told him, "If you move again I'm going to throw you off of here." They frisked us, assuming yet again that we were the ones who had robbed this woman, who probably had left her wallet at the office and needed someone to blame for her own lack of foresight.

People will use any authority to try to get their belongings back and will always assume that someone else stole them instead. I once had a party where a woman searched my entire house looking for her phone and was about to ask me to look through other people's bags and pockets until she realized in her drunken stupor that she had tucked it in her bra.

Over the years, in Brooklyn, I have seen multiple murders and been accosted by police more times than I can count. When living in Washington, DC, while attending Howard University, I was returning from a wedding sitting in the back of a van wearing a tuxedo, when the police stopped the van and accosted myself and my brother with guns drawn, even admitting that he was so scared that he "almost shot us."

I lived in New York again for a few more years, but the last straw for me there was the taxis. I had an office on Thirtieth Street and Eighth

Avenue and would sometimes go to the corner to catch a cab. Countless times white people would just walk twenty feet in front of me, and taxis would repeatedly pass me to pick them up. Sometimes there would be gracious whites who would feel sorry for me and let me take their taxi. It would be very humiliating after a hard day of work, knowing that I was probably earning more money than most of the people who were getting preferential treatment over me and usually would give the driver a bigger tip. I finally learned to form relationships with uptown car services that would take me to and from work.

One bitterly cold day, my usual livery drivers were busy working uptown, and I wound up in the cold with taxis passing me by one by one with no one in them, picking up anyone but me. Finally a driver decided to stop.

When we were two blocks away from my house in Harlem, a police car pulled up and waved the driver over. An officer came to the window and asked me for ID, then told me to get out of the car. It seems they were now looking for someone who was robbing taxis in my area. Yet again, I was the most likely suspect to be stop, frisked, asked about my whereabouts, and humiliated. My recourse would be to argue or otherwise resist, which would doubtless lead to my being arrested—or shot and killed on the street.

The next day I was walking to the subway when two cops jumped out with guns in hand, screaming for me to get against the wall. I happened to hear someone on his walkie-talkie say, "Subject is number one male 5'9", with a bald head." There I was, all 6'2" of me, with long hair down my back. They eventually let me pass.

It was at this point that I decided I needed to make a change. I had to find someplace that was more comfortable for me. A few weeks later, I got a call to work on a record in Los Angeles. I went from –20° wind chill to 80° at my Hollywood hotel. I marveled at the amount of space and the beautiful weather. New York was no longer for me.

I don't go out much. I feel safer being creative at home where I built my recording studio. At some point, we all have to find what environment works for us. I do miss many things about New York, but I am glad I have found a home someplace where I feel much safer from walking that thin line. Even so, as a Black man in America— and every Black person knows this—nowhere is truly safe, which compounds the stress of merely being human and alive in a difficult time.

1. *Curate your news. Do not sit and watch an endless feed of protests, police brutality, racism, and racial trauma.*

2. *Take social media breaks, even if it is just for an hour a day.*

3. *Use social media wisely. Don't allow it to use you. Look at your feed: is it positive and uplifting, or not? Check in on how you feel as you scroll. Take a moment to randomly stop on a post in your feed. How does that post make you feel? After you do this a few times, calculate in your mind if you have more positive or more negative feelings. Allow that to guide your decision in changing up who you follow.*

4. *Use your social media feed to follow account aligned with your values and new mantras you've learned from reading this booklet and listening to this album.*

I want to bring you back to one of the songs that I think can really help you here. "I am Powerful."

—Dr. Alfiee

I read every day online about the sheer exhaustion Black people are feeling in regard to the daily atrocities we are seeing on television and on social media. Every event seems to tap into our very soul, leaving us either seething in anger or demanding retribution that often never arrives.

Always remember that life does not solely exist in the digital world. Life is not only onscreen. Life is in connecting with your friends or family, going for a walk, or spending some time on the beach. Life is present in the simplest things: the making of a meal, or a long, hot bath.

Walk away! You don't have to wait and see what is coming next or run to your phone every five minutes to refresh a feed that will only have the same disturbing images.

THE DAILY RACIAL VIOLENCE OF TELEVISION

The murder of George Floyd, seen again and again on television and social media, was the single most impactful moment in the history of the internet.

The televising of murders was once considered to be an extremely taboo act. There was once a film company that made movies featuring live footage of murders and killings called Faces of Death, which was marked "for adults only" and held in a curtained section of video stores. As Black men and women, we often wonder: Why is it okay to show the murders of African Americans on television and not okay to show any other race or even a cat or dog being killed?

Human beings are basically empathetic and sympathetic.

Over the last few years, we have been forced to watch the brutal murders of people like Eric Garner and Philando Castile, who was shot in his car as a young girl attempted to soothe her crying and terrified mother in the back seat.

Watching Ahmaud Arbery being gunned down by men in a pickup truck made me sick

to watching these murders and executions strips us of our power. As Black men, where do we stand against a system that will allow this to happen and usually not even punish men who jump out of cars and shoot twelve-year old Black kids, and who even repeatedly punch black grandmothers in the face on the sides of highway roads. My

stomach, but then watching George Floyd being choked to

death while begging for his mother hit peak levels of American atrocity.

The first thought I had was, how do you process this? How do you not want to strike back, to bring violence and mayhem to the people who just demonstrated a completely cavalier attitude toward a Black life, knowing if it were a dog, that dog would have been allowed to live?

Watching these murders and executions strips us of our power. As Black men, where do we stand against a system that will allow this to happen and usually not even punish men who jump out of cars and shoot twelve-year old Black kids, and who even repeatedly punch black grandmothers in the face on the sides of highway roads.

WE ARE POWERFUL

Regardless of the moment, we remain infinitely powerful and connected to a divine source. We must always remember that we are made of stars and connected to universe with billions of years of history coursing through our DNA. We have the power to make change. We have the creative power to manifest a new destiny.

We can only control what is in our world. What is on the television or on social media is an outside force. Always be aware that by simply turning it off, your world will be your world at that moment.

That is where you can use your mind, intellect, and imagination to connect with your higher self. Take a moment to realize that you are a divine energy, beautiful magnificent, and glowing with an eternal sun soul.

For me, I feel like the creation of hip-hop and its becoming the most dominant and copied sound and style on the planet is an expression of musical and spiritual greatness. My personal affirmation of power is my song "I Am Powerful."

I AM POWERFUL
I AM POWERFUL
I AM POWERFUL
NOTHING CAN STOP ME
AND YOU

I AM POWERFUL

I think you read about me.

Cause you can't stop me

Cause I'm too quick you can't get the drop on me

Or put the locks on me

I'm like Tyson if the world try to box on me

I'm like a lion when a fox try to fox on me

Dahomey tribe in the Amazon rocks with me

The big homies on the docks and at the mosque homie

In the temples and the churches we the Ark homie

We save souls we the Black patriarchs homie

The Universe came from us we the spark homie

Then we brung it to the parks in the dark homie

And made hip hop the big mothership hop

The wheel within a wheel hop

Ezekiel Steel hop that don't stop

Grandmaster Flash in the park in the dark bop

Jazzy Jay back in the day on the wheels of steel

Cold Crush Brothers Double Trouble was the real deal

Romantic Fantastic with the mass appeal

We made the Wild Style brought it to the Wild Childs

To this day we still the ghost of the Mau Mau

African Kings and Queens at The Pow Wow
I'm the ghost of the Creek and the Choctaw
The ghost of the Cherokee and Bilal Rabah
Once a slave born in Mecca but now Alpha and
Omega Gave birth to King music with a record
fader

Black and holy, adorned with gold bars and
Roleys, Talking 'bout royalty with the room
smoky,
I'm the Olmec head and the God Loki
Shango the real Thor stop the okie dokie
Miriam Makeba bops and her man Stokely
Minister of the Party and it's never over
Pendulum swings back brings the power closer
Everybody just returns even Omarosa
Finishing right at the start like a revolution
Arrive at the start end with the same solution
You are the God Force don't stop keep producing
You are the God Force don't stop keep producing

I am powerful
I am powerful
I am powerful

Nothing can stop me and you
Nothing can stop me and you
Nothing can stop me and you

To start this hypothesis who built the holy properties
Who's the God force foretold in the prophecies
We the ones that made the triangle isosceles
Taught Hippocrates the Greek philosophies
And bought forth the sacred geometries
And you gotta listen this is sonic physics
It's ironic it's the sonics that Dre featured soon after the Chronic
Alicia Keys harmonics Eminem iconics
Anthony Hamilton Charlene about economics
I make opera now my tones are big symphonics
I'm the Black game of thrones Black Bolt from the comics
I'm the master of divine sound electronics

One thing I promise
When it comes to knowledge
Give me a visit I'll bless you in a minute or

An instant just like Nas did it
Just like God it
With the holy spirit ain't that picture vivid
Don't you feel you reached the limit from
what you just witnessed What you think you
gonna need for you to reach fulfillment
Pyramids are right here but your mind is
distant
Don't believe the hype you are pure spirit
You can see across a vast space
You was always first and never last place
Surpass faith come first in the last race
Set a fast pace you are powerful beloved
You the God Face

I am powerful
I am powerful
I am powerful
Nothing can stop me and you
Nothing can stop me and you
Nothing can stop me and you

I WANT TO SEE
YOU SHINING

It was March 15, 2020, and the pandemic was creeping up on the world. On that Saturday evening, I went to a dinner to celebrate the birthday of the great Elaine Brown, who is a magnificent, powerful, and respected leader who has dedicated her entire adult life to Black freedom, justice, and liberation.

I sat with her and friends as they discussed their lives as the leadership of the Black Pan-ther Party during its height. We ate great food, we laughed, we drank, and we celebrated the life of a civil rights pioneer who is just as important, if not more so, than Dr. Martin Luther King Jr. himself.

We partied on through the scare of the pandemic, and then we returned to our homes. Little did I know that it would be months before I would leave my home again.

At first it was the scare of the coronavirus, as news of sickness and deaths began to fill the news and social media timelines. I processed this fear and concern for my family, but continued on in my daily work and Zoom meetings and conferences.

Then the virus became specific, as the news began to emerge that African Americans were three to five times more likely to die from the virus, and that in some ways it was specifically targeting Black people as its primary goal of destruction.

I resisted the fear, as I began to receive calls from terrified friends, sitting in their homes, hoping and waiting that the biblical angel of death would pass over them as it did in the times of Moses. Prayers were offered, theories stated. Perhaps we were being hunted and this was a bioweapon. At first we discussed whether it was caused because of the preexisting health conditions of so many people of color, and then whether the virus was targeting people with vitamin D deficiencies, something that is prevalent in the Black community, where people have to take in twice as much sunlight to get the daily required dose.

With that came more press, more news, more social media on the frailty of Black bodies and the ongoing societal hunt that seemed to be consistently driving the demise and destruction of anyone with brown skin.

Then came the videos of the beatings by police for social distancing violations, with Black people beaten with nightsticks in front of stores, in front of their homes, and even at funerals.

The anxiety, anger, and feelings of being overwhelmed were building daily. Then came the videos of white men literally hunting a Black man, Ahmaud Arbery, gunning him down in the street as if he were a deer or a raccoon. Then we received the information that Ahmaud's murder happened months earlier, and if a video hadn't been released to the public, we would have never known about this murder. The killers that we clearly watched murder an unarmed Black man out jogging were already found to be innocent. We were angered to realize that the perpetrators of this callous and atrocious crime had already received clemency from the local police and district attorney, and that the only thing that caused their arrest was that they so reveled in the excitement and murder of a Black man that they were exposed through the gleeful sharing of the video with friends and family and the posting of images of the murder on Snapchat.

The anxiety of the powerlessness and anger amplified. We were trapped in our homes with the fear of a deadly viral ghost floating through the air, and we were forced to watch Ahmaud's murder again and again. But no, that was not going to be enough.

After months of lockdown, no gymnasium, no sporting events, no movies, no clubs, no bars, and no church, after months of hearing our family members in tears about the deaths of their friends and other relations, after hearing of bodies stacking up in morgues and relatives and not being able to visit dying family in the hospital or to grieve them at funerals, after months of not being able to console our loved ones with a simple hug, in came the delivery of the 2020 coup de grâce.

For one week straight, we had to stay indoors in our homes and repeatedly watch the choking murder of George Floyd on every news outlet and every form of social media. We watched in horror as the hunt for Black bodies reached its apex, a government official, sworn in with a badge of honor, callously choking a Black man to death with his knee in front of our eyes for nine minutes.

It is absolutely no wonder at all that the entire world snapped.

As our people burned cities and destroyed properties, my only prayer was that one day, when this was all done, that we could find a way to empower ourselves and defiantly return to this society somehow healed from this brutal psychic onslaught.

As Black people, the news and these videos stripped so much of our power away at a time when we needed it the most: for health, for strength, and for boosting our immune systems against the virus that was affecting us in disproportionate numbers. The damage of revisiting a lifetime of racial issues comes with a daily toll. Every day, I now see messages from friends on my timelines, beaten, exhausted, and drained to their last angry drop. We go back daily in our memory banks and relive passed racial atrocities, and then our very DNA goes back even further, reliving atrocities unimaginable that were epigenetically born into our consciousness.

Mental health and physical health are closely linked. When a person feels happy, divine, or blessed, they have that much more of an opportunity for their immune system to work property. Studies have shown that the body responds very well to positive thoughts during times of physical health crisis, promoting the production of happiness-inducing endorphins.

I see a mental health crisis coming in the Black community that will possibly rival the current physical health crisis. So many of our beautiful Black people have been under extreme pressure for an extraordinary amount of time.

Today, many Black people not only feel over-whelmed by the disproportionate number of casualties from the current virus, but also the grief and anguish from the loss of close friends and family members.

If you add to that grief, despair, and terror the feelings of anger and outrage from so many recent episodes of hatred and violence, already overwhelming thoughts have begun to grow to a level of physical and mental stress that will be beyond what many people can handle. This will yield even more deadly results.

With this in mind, as an elder statesman in hip-hop culture and the music industry as a whole, I have decided to share my offering of the affirmations I recorded during the days from March 15 to June 15, 2020, recordings I created to balance the onslaught and negative psychic energy that I was bombarded with during those months. It was these recordings that helped me to exercise and make healthy diet choices over alcohol, drugs, and binge eating, helped me to negate the fear, loss, anger, and feelings of outrage that

assaulted my body and soul daily during the entire time. In essence, these recordings were integral in my keeping my health and sanity intact. I dropped twenty pounds during that time, and when bombarded with negative I can hear the recorded song affirmations bouncing around my head, drowning out and then pushing away the negativity. I can see the words boosting my mind when I wake up in the morning. During that time, I let three of the people closest to me listen to the recordings, and they all reported a glowing sensation, feeling uplifted and energized.

I am loved and not hunted. I can breathe. My lungs are superstrong. I am powerful. I am strong and courageous. I have no fear. I control fear. I'm above fear. I am successful. My body is a temple in perfect health. These have been my daily affirmations. Even if you are in prison, or in a hospital, you are more beautiful with every second, and omniscient.

You are beautiful. I want to see you shining.

Affirm every day. Erase the negative programming that these disgusting social media videos and pictures are presenting. You are not hated, you are not a victim. Quite the contrary: you are divine, you are magnificent, you are powerful, you are royalty. Find a royal name for yourself. Say it to yourself in the mirror. Remind yourself every day that you are beautiful, that you are loved, and in the realization of your unique and divine greatness, that you have no fear.

Onward!

Mark Batson
a.k.a.
King Batson the First

THE LYRICS

I AM

(repeat after me)

I AM
I AM

I'm a walking monument to excellence
I'm a higher force of being
I'm the pinnacle of universal intelligence
I'm the living biblical testament

It's not arrogance when you're living proof of the evidence
When the God force surrounds you
and you fulfilled all the prerequisites

I now admonish decadence and make a new precedent

My body is full of life force and now higher forces are blessing it
The holy spirit refreshing it
I'm feeling it all up inside of my chest and s***

There's no energy that can defeat me, beat me,
sit me down or hold me back
All attacks are like Neo when he waved them bullets,
Devils is shooting at me crooked
And shocked to see me still standing
Grandmaster Commanding with enough passion to
fill up the Grand Canyon

I'm the equivalent of a 100-man battalion
Take out a general with prayers from my candles
Wave my hand and watch the enemy fall
While I'm wearing sandals
They shooting rifles but the God force done broke they ankles,

I'm a Wooly Mammoth, 10 tons of Gods' Commandments
Sit me with you chaplains and your preachers
for some holy understanding Knowledge,
wisdom with the God force inside my system
This is our future look at this man right here after the sun done
kissed him.

I'm the epitome of Vitamin D
You might even see, a spiritual light force in the presence of me
In whispered tones they mentioning me,

Ain't that that royal King with no bling
Who went on to these spiritually higher things

Watch a phoenix rise from the ashes
Tasting like grandma's glass molasses
Mixed with Grandmaster Flash's scratches.

Resist all their military advances
Whether physical or biological
I'm still standing here with perfect balance
They fear me, because no matter what happens I remain in action,
I easily pay their taxes and bypass economic sanctions,
And continue manifesting in manufacturing
Holy verses that feed the famine
While fashionably kicking it in my mansion
So get my name right not like Steve Harvey in them pageants.
King Batson I'm the nephew of Action Jackson,
A little bit of Mr. T my songs get Clubber Lang reactions
A little bit of Mr. T my songs get Clubber Lang reactions.

Because I AM

I AM

AFFIRMATIONS

What you think you will become
What you dream will be the words from your tongue
Which will manifest and never be undone
What you teach will one day be the songs that are sung
Powerful and towering like the breath inside your lungs
Just for fun
Imagine you're at the center of the Sun you are One
Unlimited and forever young
What we do we put the Fu in Kung the Chi in Tai,
By being born spirits that will never die forever fly
There's no earthly measure that measures these holy treasures of I

Affirmations
These are the words that built mighty nations,
These are the thoughts that brought forth God's Creations
That taught source code to generations
Graduate degrees in radiation
It was these very powerful words that was the foundation

Consider this your freshman orientation
An invitation to be on the God Force Delegation
Where you are Unlimited with no limitations

Consider this your divine coronation
And entrance into an infinity nation

Everything built once has been built twice
First the thought in your mind brings the structure to life
Then the vocalizing to the word emphasizes the thought and
And brings the thought to light
Can you see it just tell me you want to be it

Convince yourself you are the conduit and then
Make that energy light fluid.

Affirmations

I have the freedom to create the world I desire
My possibilities are endless I'm a holy fire
I make all my dreams come true
I'm the story writer
I love myself and my whole entire being
I'm seeing I'm now testifying and achieving higher.

I trust my intuition and trust all my decisions
I stay focused with precision
Making the most of my self supervision

Affirmations

MASTERING FEAR

I am strong and courageous I'm above fear
I am strong and courageous I control fear
I am strong and courageous I have no fear

My confidence in my abilities

Has no fragilities

Since I stepped into divine nobility

I'm royalty I'm royalty

You see me on a throne

Made of alabaster stone

Risen from a Madagascar tomb

Elevated to a Master Room

Graduated to I became immune

My spirit warriors are a God Platoon

Originated from a dark cocoon

Elevated to the sun and moon

Mahdi like the son in Dune

I am the spice the divine perfume that permeates

the holy room (Ittar)

I won like Kobe do like Obi Do
Won Kenobi in eternity holy you
Gon' know me too
Pedagogy like a Yogi too pedagogy teaching the homies too
Rituals and ceremonies boo plus coming home with the trophy too

Look In my eyes closely and slowly too
Look in my eyes beloved and see what the Sankofe do
Some nights and days I know it might get lonely to
But on those nights remember there's a Godly soul in You

Hindus wear a Tupi do, Muslims a Kufi do,
in Judaism there's a Kufi too,
Christianity there's a priestly hood that shows the good,
But the inner religion is in what you do,
how you live, how you give,
How you humble yourself and you learn to forgive, and outlive,
And suddenly you mastered how to master fear
I have mastered how to master fear
I have mastered how to master fear

No Fear

(repeat)

I LOVE WORKING OUT

I love working out King
More excited than ever for me to make it to the gym Queen
I'm on the swim team muscle on the slim team
Love working out King Love working out queen
More excited than ever to make it to the gym lean
Slim on the weight machine
Grim on the great machines,
Do the leg raise machine,
Treadmills and plate machines
Body annihilate I drop weight and break machines
Put the whole rack on,
Strap it to my back on,
I'm military obligatory get my lumberjack on
Knock down a few trees getting my quarterback on
Take on the whole team getting my running back on
Bodies are grabbing me I'm pulling the whole pack on
More bodies they stack on I'm carrying the Razorbacks home
This ain't no time to relax at home
I'm doing grips of flips till I eclipse the throne

I WANT TO SEE YOU SHINING

I want to
see you shining
golden lights
silver lining
always climbing
stars aligning
royal life
so exciting
fine dining
So inspired
you invited
so excited

window seat
see us flying
all day
prophesizing
see the future
ain't it bright and
full of hope I'm
testifying

book signing
strobe lights
disco nights
soar to heights
knowing we are
synthesizing
connected to these
sources higher
shining on us
holy fire
live forever
never tired
but entitled
dream bigger
be enlightened
confident with
senses heightened
the only thing we
know is triumph
the only thing we know is triumph
the only thing we know is triumph

I AM SO SUCCESSFUL

Good morning everybody
I am so successful
Good morning my love
I am so successful
Good morning baby I said
I am so successful
Good morning baby I said
I am so successful

You got to have some success in your projections
It starts with the words and successful interjections
Meditate on those and then some introspection
Even Jesus said I am resurrecting
He wouldn't have got up on that cross with no protection
If every day you embracing your oppression
Being a victims 'gon be your next obsession
'Gon have to change that if you want to live in Heaven

I look in the mirror and I know that I'm blessed
And I look again and I say thank you thank God for my success
I look in the mirror and I know that I'm blessed
And I look again and I say thank you thank God for my success

Thank you thank you God for all of my success yes
Thank you thank you God for all of my success yes

Ate my vegetables then I went to festivals
Drank my water saying damn I'm so successful

I ain't victimized that world will have you hypnotized
I'm the God of my universe I clearly have identified
I control who's chastised and I control who's glorified
Of any other bullshit I will not be preoccupied
I am the Beatitudes my blessings are personified
Come with negativity you'll quickly be disqualified

Wow its sunny
Look at that honey
Ain't our God also the God of money

I look in the mirror and I know that I'm blessed
And I look again and I say thank you thank God for my success
I look in the mirror and I know that I'm blessed
And I look again and I say thank you thank God for my success
Thank You Thank you God for all of my Success Yes
Thank You Thank you God for all of my Success Yes

I ain't victimized that world will have you hypnotized
I'm the God of my universe I clearly have identified
I control who's chastised and I control who's glorified
Of any other bullshit I will not be preoccupied
God is my granddaddy so I got the God vibes
Will you take his name and be God personified

Good morning everybody
I am so successful
Good morning my love
I am so successful
Good morning baby I said
I am so successful
Good morning baby I said
I am so successful

YOU ARE ELEGANT

Mirror work I tell you that it really works
Take off your shirt if you have to say it you perfect first
I see a burst of pride inside your eyes behind the lies and hurt
It's no surprise you are perfected styles of earth and dirt
Mold your clay you younger you not old today
Holiday perfection for your body is
Just a goal away
But first we have to say that we're perfect today
And every day we're getting better and better in every way,
You are elegant
Every other thought is irrelevant
Born to be an angel you are heaven sent

You are elegant
Every other thought is irrelevant
Born to be an angel you are heaven sent

When I'm around you
I'm so glad I finally found you
I finally hear you

I don't fear you when I'm in the mirror
I see you clearer and now I want to be you bigger
Elevate my vision of precision and then make it fiercer

I am elegant
I'm getter better I'm perfecting
I am elegant
I'm getting better I'm perfecting

It is evident I'm chosen a divine selection
Every possible blessing is headed straight in my direction

Come on over dance a little bossa nova
The greatest dancer of all time is in the mirror sober
Get some closure on the joker who told you you was lower
Put the vision of you higher up on a movie poster
You the owner of your image and the soul controller
Take a polaroid and tape it on your toaster and get to boasting
You are solar, nothing about you is mediocre
You're the broker of this real estate so make it doper

I AM POWERFUL

I think you read about me.

Cause you can't stop me

Cause I'm too quick you can't get the drop on me

Or put the locks on me

I'm like Tyson if the world try to box on me

I'm like a lion when a fox try to fox on me

Dahomey tribe in the Amazon rocks with me

The big homies on the docks and at the mosque homie

In the temples and the churches we the Ark homie

We save souls we the Black patriarchs homie

The Universe came from us we the spark homie

Then we brung it to the parks in the dark homie

And made hip hop the big mothership hop

The wheel within a wheel hop

Ezekiel Steel hop that don't stop

Grandmaster Flash in the park in the dark bop

Jazzy Jay back in the day on the wheels of steel

Cold Crush Brothers Double Trouble was the real deal

Romantic Fantastic with the mass appeal

We made the Wild Style brought it to the

Wild Childs To this day we still the ghost of the Mau Mau

African Kings and Queens at The Pow Wow

I'm the ghost of the Creek and the Choctaw
The ghost of the Cherokee and Bilal Rabah
Once a slave born in Mecca but now Alpha and Omega
Gave birth to King music with a record fader

Black and holy, adorned with gold bars and Roleys,
Talking 'bout royalty with the room smoky,

I'm the Olmec head and the God Loki
Shango the real Thor stop the okie dokie
Miriam Makeba bops and her man Stokely
Minister of the Party and it's never over
Pendulum swings back brings the power closer
Everybody just returns even Omarosa
Finishing right at the start like a revolution
Arrive at the start end with the same solution
You are the God Force don't stop keep producing
You are the God Force don't stop keep producing

I am powerful
I am powerful
I am powerful
Nothing can stop me and you
Nothing can stop me and you
Nothing can stop me and you

To start this hypothesis who built the holy properties
Who's the God force foretold in the prophecies
We the ones that made the triangle isosceles
Taught Hippocrates the Greek philosophies
And bought forth the sacred geometries
And you gotta listen this is sonic physics
It's ironic it's the sonics that Dre featured soon after the
Chronic Alicia Keys harmonics Eminem iconics
Anthony Hamilton Charlene about economics
I am make opera now my tones are big symphonics
I'm the Black game of thrones Black Bolt from the comics
I'm the master of divine sound electronics

One thing I promise
When it comes to knowledge
Give me a visit I'll bless you in a minute or
An instant just like Nas did it
Just like God it
With the holy spirit ain't that picture vivid
Don't you feel you reached the limit from what you just witnessed
What you think you gonna need for you to reach fulfillment
Pyramids are right here but your mind is distant
Don't believe the hype you are pure spirit
You can see across a vast space

You was always first and never last place
Surpass faith come first in the last race
Set a fast pace you are powerful beloved
You the God Face

I am powerful
I am powerful
I am powerful
Nothing can stop me and you
Nothing can stop me and you
Nothing can stop me and you

YOU ARE BEAUTIFUL

Time is always passing there's another lesson
Life is full of memories and many recollections
And every time I recognize you are a better blessing
You are beautiful more beautiful with every second
You are beautiful more beautiful with every second
We must respect it in these monuments that are erected
Forever protect it as we manifest that time is just a lesson
We getting younger daily that's my main intention

But after this we have a kiss and then a resurrection
We master this and after this we are divine reflections
Universal soul beings with divine perception
Three sixty degrees of knowledge we achieve perfection

We are more than these physical beings
Much more than this physical form we visiting on
Live every day like it's our first we are unlimited born,
Brand new every day as our souls put on this physical uniform

(repeat—build twice)

You are beautiful more beautiful with every second
You are beautiful more beautiful with every second
You are beautiful more beautiful with every second
You are beautiful more beautiful with every second

Time has no limitations and no directions
All that matters with time is that we do respect it
And I respect you cause your presence healed me of depression
The right person can you give you perspective and divine
direction

You are beautiful more beautiful with every second
You are beautiful more beautiful with every second
You are beautiful more beautiful with every second
You are beautiful more beautiful with every second

MY BODY IS A TEMPLE

My body is temple I'm in perfect health
My body is temple I'm in perfect heath
I'm stronger than these man-made diseases
These heathens can't win for any reasons
The next 200 seasons the God force allegiance
Uniting all colors Polynesians to Indonesians
I'll bridge the Africans and Europeans
The same way the Egyptians taught the alphabet to the
Phoenicians And culturally speaking
It's the Nubians that taught the Greeks and Roman philosophies
and Our only reasons
Was for us to unite the whole planet and make
it healthy for a million seasons

My body is temple I'm in perfect health
My body is temple I'm in perfect heath
End of every season I'm fasting it's pleasing
Enhancing my vision and my breathing on every evening
You probably won't ever hear me sneezing
My lungs are so strong I blow a breeze and you start freezing

My body is a temple I'm in perfect health
My body is a temple I'm in perfect heath

No emergencies just vitamin Cs and Ds
And some sea moss seaweed from the 7 seas algaes On
42nd Street I used to blow the weeds,
Now it's mullein leaves mixed with the black seed

My body is a temple I'm in perfect health
My body is a temple I'm in perfect heath

CELEBRATE THE VICTORY

I have
Achieved the victory
I was born victorious
Yes I always victorious
Universal glorious

Celebrate   with   me   the
victory   Celebrate   with
me the victory

The sun of stars
Blessings to the life of the Gods
The wisdoms and earths who gave birth from the hurt and the
dirt
In divine spurts.
Raised in the water in the womb our divine church
This water been here for a billion years that I was made up
I was prayed up from stardust I'm ancient
I'm almighty God force sanctioned
I'm the sun of the raisin of Langston
Hughes the son of Rastafarians born in Kingston
Jamaican irie Kings wearing Halle Selassie rings while Empress
Selassie sings Virtuoso martini and Rossi with the glossy things

CELEBRATE THE VICTORY

Hot as the saucy wings around your mouth
Leaving a mark like a frothy coffee ring
Big Tings and dem bring kings to dem and
queens playing strings to dem symphony sings to dem
I'm a piano playing poet from the projects a picturesque player who
pound for pound gets
poom poom and protects
I soon soon do expect that you too
will make the big big giant move for respect
But it starts with self
Raise your hands in victory you are the epitome for infinity
You are the epitome for infinity
You are a holy powerful universal star child entity
With an eternal love cosmic Identity
A thousand lifetimes just to get to the right times
Lessons to be blessings your future
Identity mind in the future when
your stars align in the grand spirit design
A close encounter of the original kind
One with the Universe with your eternal divinity mind
You are magnificent I am magnificent every time
You are magnificent I am magnificent in every way for all time.

You get it now.
There's nothing that can stop us or stand in our way.
We are so powerful.
Universal eternal light energy forces.
Living in bodies of water as God's sons and daughters.
Every day is a victory.

Claim it
It's yours
This is our world we can make it whatever we want it to be
Take a deep breath and say
I am the One
I am the One
I am magnificent
I am fantastic
I am powerful
I am strong, healthy, and magnificent
Nothing can stand in my way
Say it
VICTORY
Victory, Victory, Victory

You are a holy powerful universal star child entity
With an eternal love cosmic Identity
A thousand lifetimes just to get to the right times
Lessons to be blessings your future

Identity mind in the future when

your stars align in the grand spirit design

A close encounter of the original kind

One with the Universe with your eternal divinity mind

You are magnificent I am magnificent every time

You are magnificent I am magnificent in every way for all time.

You get it now.

There's nothing that can stop us or stand in our way.

We are so powerful.

Universal eternal light energy forces.

Living in bodies of water as God's sons and daughters.

Every day is a victory.

Claim it

It's yours

This is our world we can make it whatever we want it to be

Take a deep breath and say

I am the One

I am the One

I am magnificent

I am fantastic

I am powerful

I am strong, healthy, and magnificent

Nothing can stand in my way

Say it

VICTORY

Victory, Victory, Victory

A COLORING BOOK

Not too many years ago, I was going through a stressful time. I went to see my sister, Cara, who has been an elementary school teacher for almost thirty years. She sat me down with a coloring book, and I colored with a crayon in between the lines for the first time since I was a kid. It was more stress-relieving than I could have possibly imagined. I have included two sets of images to color.

The first five are big smiles: I Want to See You Shining.

The second five are called Celebrating the Victory.

RESOURCES

AAKOMA PROJECT, INC

The AAKOMA Project has many initiatives, including free virtual therapy for young Black people, teens of color, and marginalized youth.

www.aakomaproject.org

571.486.3382

MENTAL HEALTH COALITION

The Mental Health Coalition (MHC) believes we must increase the conversation around mental health. Visit the MHC Resource Library made available by their alliance of the leading mental health organizations to find support.

https://thementalhealthcoalition.org/resources/

TEENLINE

A teen to teen hotline that youth worldwide can call/text/email to talk about their struggles

www.teenlineonline.org

CALL: I-800-852-8336

TEXT: TEEN to 839863

Made in the USA
Monee, IL
09 April 2022

94396674R00044